KNOWING WON'T LET DARKNESS REIGN

BOOKS BY MARTIN JANELLO

LIVE KNOWING LIFE
ISBN 978-0-9910649-6-0 (Paperback)
ISBN 978-0-9983020-2-7 (Kindle)

LOVE KNOWING LOVE
ISBN 978-0-9910649-7-7 (Paperback)
ISBN 978-0-9983020-3-4 (Kindle)

PINE KNOWING PAIN
ISBN 978-0-9910649-5-3 (Paperback)
ISBN 978-0-9983020-6-5 (Kindle)

SHINE KNOWING SHAME
ISBN 978-0-9983020-4-1 (Paperback)
ISBN 978-0-9983020-7-2 (Kindle)

CLIMB KNOWING AIM
ISBN 978-0-9983020-5-8 (Paperback)
ISBN 978-0-9983020-8-9 (Kindle)

KNOWING WON'T LET DARKNESS REIGN
ISBN 978-0-9983020-1-0 (Paperback)
ISBN 978-0-9983020-9-6 (Kindle)

PHILOSOPHY OF HAPPINESS
ISBN 978-0-9910649-0-8 (Hardcover)
ISBN 978-0-9910649-8-4 (Paperback, Pt. 1)
ISBN 978-0-9910649-9-1 (Paperback, Pt. 2)
ISBN 978-0-9910649-1-5 (PDF E-book)
ISBN 978-0-9910649-2-2 (Kindle)
ISBN 978-0-9910649-3-9 (EPUB)

PHILOSOPHIC REFLECTIONS
ISBN 978-0-9910649-4-6 (PDF E-book)

KNOWING WON'T LET DARKNESS REIGN

PHILOSOPHICAL QUOTES & POEMS

MARTIN JANELLO

Copyright © 2020 by Martin Janello

All rights reserved

No part of this book may be reproduced or transmitted,
in any form or by any means, electronic,
mechanical, or otherwise,
without prior written permission from its copyright owner

Cover, book design, and artwork by Martin Janello

Published by Palioxis Publishing

Palioxis, Palioxis Publishing,
and the Palioxis Publishing colophon
are trademarks owned by Martin Janello

Publisher website:
www.palioxis.com

Book website:
www.philosophyofhappiness.com

ISBN 978-0-9983020-1-0

First Edition

CONTENTS

I. STASIS AND UNREST	1
II. INIQUITY AND DECEIT	23
III. SECRET AND SACRED	45
IV. SOME TIME AGO	63
V. FRAME OF MIND	83
VI. CRITIQUE	117
VII. DESPAIR	137
VIII. REGRET	163
IX. ANTICIPATION	185
X. HEALING	211

This book is dedicated

to

those who

won't let

darkness reign

I.
STASIS
AND
UNREST

2 *KNOWING WON'T LET DARKNESS REIGN*

I. STASIS AND UNREST

we are not responsible

for our dreams

that is why we hesitate

making them come true

i think you are changing my dna

strands once securely tied

open in fray

searching to find yours

it's not the tasks you do

tiring leaching you out

rather what you can't move

carries that draining clout

she had him praying to lose himself
drown helpless in lovelorn devotion
sensing his pain
she parked him on a shelf
with melancholy as stand-in emotion

hearts are made of rubber bands
tugging parts departed close
no matter how far or where it ends

i want to be so perfect for you
that i can't live down my being not
rather would see you missing my cue
than let you befrown what i have got

I. STASIS AND UNREST

by presence and absence
alternatively confined
in seen and unseen aspects
these make us change our mind
ending this seesaw is underlined

life seems like a race
she's always so busy
makes herself dizzy
by trying to brace
for the frustration of treading in place

natural process or artifice
cannot decide which we prefer

dreams of happy lives
once they'd have a car
labored and deprived
summers of their youths
never made it that far
stalled for tolls at booths

bemoaning lack of traction
heading for nowhere we want to go

much love i hear
dims past its season
but that depends upon its reason
or the lack thereof

I. STASIS AND UNREST

quaint alleys carry

on worn travertine

passing joy heaviness and trifle

never accedes to suggestions

without belief

they arose in her mind

can't let go anything

without questions

to relieve fear of what she may find

sleep they say

is training for death

most of us already loathing to wake

life's like a house prone

to water mains breaking

we better dwell on higher ground

once we thrive

on vicarious thrill

we feel alive

though we're standing still

is she inspired

or merely possessed

she's never tired

or easy at rest

most alive contrast to dying

I. STASIS AND UNREST

my mind has you pegged
as a girl too long-legged
for wanting to stay in place

the struggler who's
sick of a humdrum life
still too afraid to leave the hive

waves of music love and wine
daring to sway
while standing grounded
clocks tick loudly protesting time
he's still wondering
stays confounded

10 *KNOWING WON'T LET DARKNESS REIGN*

let's sail somewhere
that is not here
away from the anchors
we forged and threw

too many memories
raw unsurpassed
safe from all elegies
fates to be cast

she's letting him repeatedly know
he's not enthusiastic enough
each demerit feels like a blow
betterment will be tough

I. STASIS AND UNREST

she was supposed to be
hitched by now
all her friends felt
she was failing
yet the finality
frightens somehow
even at risk of flailing

my monkey lives not
in branches of trees
it sits on my neck
prepared to raise heck
should it suspect
i'm losing track
or not react
to what it sees

that we subsist
on shreds of hope
is not a noble strength

she cries
i cannot go on anymore
want instead ever to stay

went to the fair on my own dare
trying to get affected
drown in the crowd
laughing without care
silent in loud you just stood there
kindred souls detected

I. STASIS AND UNREST

the older the world
the more difficult
being an original

resign and re-sign
a dance card
with crossed-out
and newfangled people
sentimentality has no seat
long as the music doesn't stop

don't know how much love
is about timing
but the percentage must be high

the overdrive
he had for life
made peers
on the road seem
like they were standing

why does he feel
too exhausted to rest
spirit's an eel
and hope a pest
cannot see looking forward

waiting for death
by waiting for life

I. STASIS AND UNREST

she lights a fuse
but it's no use
missing her cues
dreams run out of time

praising how wise it is
standing your ground
you seem much less a whiz
once you have drowned

for those living well
others who are not
are frightening reminders
of their own vulnerability

KNOWING WON'T LET DARKNESS REIGN

today my love
has gotten restless
worries had built
so i could not see
no matter what
you'll be standing with me

we have to let go of everything
to move about truly free
the question that we then must ask
how free do we want to be

getting by in a field of muck
until we die or live on stuck

I. STASIS AND UNREST

rising surprising
friends who lost hope
and fiends who were gloating
you slid off the slope

all the love they make to each other
seems impromptu but is rehearsed
innocence slowly turned into bother
when they wished to be better versed

The dumber people are, the more
they think of themselves as geniuses
for realizing something they had not
known or thought of before.

trying to rouse
those ensconced in daydreams
or oblivious slumber
will likely earn their thunder

Your pursuing of visions may irritate
some people because it reminds them
of aspirations they buried alive or
never dared admitting or gestating.

wallowing daily in our bubbles
led to deny our brains are washed
taking sides as if it matters
while our lives are senselessly rushed

I. STASIS AND UNREST

the music won't stop

if you drop your coat

nor care if you like to dance

or follow its plot of cold and hot

of endless despair and romance

you're only a dot

meant to be of short note

or transient dissonance

love knows no time

so i won't hang in

waiting for you

to see if it grows

you'd get accustomed

resent or feel guilty

giving rise to intensified woes

i lost myself searching
to find the true me
nightmares were lurching
to set themselves free
like bats disturbed
in their daytime suspension

where are you
she silently asked through the ages
finally bring her to feel you are here

minds received foreign modulations
watch others do or simulations
deem them replacements for life

I. STASIS AND UNREST

living one's story against the odds
or going with the flow
compromising may serve us best
but often it's hard to know

running through empty halls
endless night castle
he once built
for a promised queen

i cherish those
who break the dull
unravel the lull
they or someone chose

how much wine
does take to believe
you are drunk on life
with no fear of love

when crepuscule paints fun a sin
and falling shadows set night to begin
play your own fool
make light from within

people may think she's unsteady
trying herself at this and at that
but how else to know she is ready
past wearing a scholar's robe and hat

II.
INIQUITY
AND
DECEIT

24 KNOWING WON'T LET DARKNESS REIGN

II. INIQUITY AND DECEIT

every election

a choice among evils

following pointless contention

nothing we're told

is how it's portrayed

claiming innocence now is too late

clinical undertow

growing with dread

some still show

naked hands and head

dress code can't quite

make them sock puppets yet

calamity real
for whom it involves
but it is contrived
by skulking wolves
so we let them run the herd

criminal minds look for justifications
the most advanced
make their victims agree

paid emoluments for hypocrisy
we still pretend our government
comes from caring democracy
bear disappointments that won't end

II. INIQUITY AND DECEIT

History and religion are propaganda by criminal syndicates. That we still fall for their cons proves we have learned little since our inception.

Public manipulation works two ways: Galvanizing a sufficient minority behind a guided scheme and keeping the majority apathetic and gullible.

Habitual parasites and abusers are usually proficient swindlers. The best paralyze victims by injecting guilt, but this is also their dead giveaway.

KNOWING WON'T LET DARKNESS REIGN

flash and swagger for vapid sway
compensation of nothing to say
all to be a célébrité
making a show with affected noise
drowning out those deprived of voice

thought police run by deputies
burning who won't succumb's effigies
all in the service of broadmindedness

hyperventilating cries
claiming higher ground
poisoned dialogue of sides
foil peace to be found

II. INIQUITY AND DECEIT

all may be lost if mobs abuse

incommodious obvious truths

fanned by interests aiming to protect

lies legitimized as politically correct

prepared to use lies

when they think they are right

anything flies to win the fight

no one has scruples any more

gleaming cars

expensive dresses

cover scars

and unseen messes

dream masters make us
believe we are awake
move life past us
so we give
and they can take

if those entrusted with our powers
do not represent us
they tend to employ diversions
commensurate with their betrayal

Giving people credible illusions of
self-determination is the most
effective way to keep them subjects.

II. INIQUITY AND DECEIT

spectacles to distract

now as then

vertebrae cracked

to keep spite in the pen

and us from finding our purpose

your head is already in the sand

all else will trail with its use at an end

issuing rules

what to think feel or say

claiming veracity

for their false way

calling us apostates

sly puppeteers
have pawns serially follow
plays of tears inherently hollow
ties on ears they mistake for free wills
they unknowingly act as shills

the liberality of most extends
as far as they get their way

unknowing pretenders
a growing group
of those duped thinking
they run the loop or at least
that they could be contenders

II. INIQUITY AND DECEIT

hypocrite outrage

by those seeking power

till they or their friends

arrive at the top

hate permission strewn as bait

captures the wrongfully righteous

to do the bidding of devils who wait

once we get hooked to bite us

every time evil

leaves its shadows

it ventures to hide

in the highest virtues

good people try
to get friendly by
that's what evil counts on

mornings we go on
about our business
ties cold to the world outside
inside thirsting
for all that glistens
rising from ambers
of fires burnt

timid bullies
wait for a mob

II. INIQUITY AND DECEIT

looking for news

to confirm opinions

slandering all

that does not fit

trustees and trustors aligned

they scare us

so we choose

the safety

they offer

zealots misguide

no matter their side

while insisting the other lied

shrill shills

pushing pills for ills

their masters manufactured

    our synapses streamlined trim

    clogged with nonsense to the brim

    that's how rulers want us

    they constantly drilled into our minds

    there are no borders no boundaries

    asked us to toss out keys and designs

    tolerant trust our ideals to foundries

    make believe evil did not exist

    or had to be taken in with the good

II. INIQUITY AND DECEIT

Human acuity is frequently corrupted by requiring compelling proof for truths one is loath to admit but none or little for convenient falsehoods.

Bad political systems make subjects believe they are too dysfunctional to improve but also that alternate forms of organization are inferior or futile.

truth at first an airy friend
gains stalling weight if we pretend
pulls us down and eats our soul
there's no escape we must pay the toll

evil has interests maintaining conflict

there are two sides to pretending
one expanding one upending
who we are

animals mimicking
fast food mascots
endless surprise and supplies

lies we tell our self when we love
and even more when we don't

II. INIQUITY AND DECEIT

few grasped at the time

falsehoods falling like snow

heralded human winter

devised diversions

from existential strife

pharmacies of entertainment

make us dwell in self-containment

not approaching real life

in our service to the hive

often the ones pointing

faults out in others

try to push their crimes under covers

her feel is electric
tight leather high heel
leaves men apoplectic
for nothing is real
android domestic violence

part of their plan is to tire us out
so we won't loudly complain
their growth is all this is about
matched by destruction and pain

trying to come into our own
or be somebody
labors surprisingly hard to distinguish

II. INIQUITY AND DECEIT

snake oiled salesmen

feelgood claims

selling our vanity

back at bazars

quicksand sculptures

few kernels of truth

then we move on

to another booth

staying terrified in herds

run by charitable words

of helpers who seem not to need us

insisting we are shrewd

but our minds are skewed

flout all signs we are to be stewed

by predators posing as leaders

the best chance these days
to be on the right track
assume opposites
of what is sold as fact

We hide parts of ourselves, fearing
others would not accept us if they
knew of them. However, this may
isolate us more, even in company.

pretense soon past tense
false advertising
still tells the truth
about backstage conditions

II. INIQUITY AND DECEIT

Success in amoral settings means one has overcome one's soul, and fighting remnants still in the way to continue being able to live with oneself.

    you tear yourself up
    getting out of the forest
    that is reliably proven a shelter
    those fairy tales should not be trusted

    dishonesties perpetrated or suffered
    once painful cuts
    are overcome now honor has gone
    accepted means for self-promotion

we're cracked eggs
eternally intrigued
by our conception
of being intact
feed on confection
moving perception
to beautiful tales
against all proof of fact

you may believe
no masters exist
through manipulation
and absence of fist
but why blow your life
playing into such risk
by conforming consumption

III.
SECRET
AND
SACRED

III. SECRET AND SACRED

today she finally noticed me
as i lingered walking by
when her glances heartened me
i wanted to turn and cry
though i am hardly a sensitive guy

with proof of no deity
would we go insane
or break out in gaiety
shedding inherent blame
free to take charge of our flame

pretend your existence is all in order
love long banned beyond the border

All the world's problems can be
traced to a preference of wanting to
believe over wanting to know.

everywhere she treads
she pulls sighs or bated breaths
causing heaves by vacuums she leaves

Ideas one can run common affairs
well without common participation
or in leader and follower settings are
sad illusions, perpetuated by laziness
and ignorance on one side and desire
for power and wealth on the other.

III. SECRET AND SACRED

say how much opinion
is based on witnessed fact
or mentalized dominion
our brains are playing back

the world may be crumbling
still don't send love tumbling
that's when it's needed the most

weakness and strength
tolerance resistance
love and hate
are varied states of the same
like vapor water and ice

you're only not free if you act like it
only not heard if you quietly sit
only oppressed giving in to it
only tied down once you commit
only entombed if you dig the pit

don't let them claim love's just for fun
after life's acts or omissions are done
and all else of our self has moved on
love may survive intact some or none
we can plan how much we'll be gone

trying to get a reading on you
love you're my fever thermometer

III. SECRET AND SACRED

mundane as usual gets a bad rap
when in fact it keeps us sober
tiding us securely over
to consider each untried act

Many human highs and lows can be
explained by our habit of wanting the
opposite of what we currently have.

she is composed
a rounded self-inspired work
he has admired numerous times
he likes it most and she tries to shirk
that her heart won't reflect his crimes

fear less fiends trying to break doors
than resentful friends
whom we let in on all fours

ungracious beauty is ugly

love is an imposition of intimacy
that only those in love will bear

the day you stop wishing
to be in someone's grace
you're free but also without love

III. SECRET AND SACRED

For interesting conversation, ask
loved ones what they would do if you
turned into a zombie.

just after i had all belief
in freeing love dismissed
i met this graceful enigmatic being
i had not dared envision to exist
calmly arresting my aimless fleeing
no more longing for relief

life's odds are stacked against us
because we play our chips
without understanding the game

secrets kept not to hurt each other
anyway debts against our love
lowering chances of being forgiven

she fell in love with him
wild and free
secretly hoping
for some lee
even as winds were changing

holding ears it goes on her nerves
when he plays rock and roll
she fears rousing the reserves
stalking her body and soul

III. SECRET AND SACRED

she sometimes says

go away to herself

mostly unsure in what ways

swiftly returns the bottle to the shelf

this battle can stretch for days

my dreams of you

were split in two

one sleeping

and one waking

words originated in sounds

things make as their composers

making them all notations of music

No La Scala without scales.

anything you put on
you pull off
including me

she is proud
without being loud
calm sunny elegance
puts everyone at ease
still be aware
if you should dare
that burning repentance
will bend your knees

III. SECRET AND SACRED

the little spark

she keeps in her heart

pilot light for fulminance

what just seems to come

to our mind

sometimes has had

hidden storied gestations

something in us keeps track

of things ugly

we make beautiful

and things beautiful

we make ugly

those visions
he does not write about
looking for ways
to materialize

You can discover a lot about yourself
and your fate by contemplating what
you keep in store for eventual use.

nothing else now matters
clasped scent of hair and skin
unqualified acceptance
not knowing who i've been
or what will be with us

III. SECRET AND SACRED

he was considered half-domesticated
ate at the sink only when she was out

passionate lovers are unprepared
so much so fast
but there's no other path

spring eve's walk
we took together
blushing glancing
unsure to say
intimate almost
like naked dancing
which still holds much future sway

It is not so much that we don't sense or could not know or find out what makes us happy. We much more hold ourselves back by fear of change succeeding or not succeeding and of what it might take to accomplish it.

making nature artifice
sacred mission
or cursed perversion

i try to catch the hush
of words that sometimes
skim my mind

III. SECRET AND SACRED

the music i write

is familiar to me

because each sound

is a note about you

what is this existence defined by roles

being a boy girl man or woman

being a couple parent sibling child

being a friend being anything

we find out

when we reflect and project love

his finer grains ground coarse

on eternity's shores

is he silent

for secrets he keeps

fear of offending

once he speaks

not being heard

or not believed

or is it for pain

that meaning will drain

by giving it name

his nightfulness ensconces you

in warm illumination

makes you undress

what you might do

devoid of trepidation

till sun breaks untamed moods

IV. SOME TIME AGO

64   *KNOWING WON'T LET DARKNESS REIGN*

IV. SOME TIME AGO

during a dance i met a girl

moving like a cat

taking a stance to give me a whirl

yet i instead of coast

stood planted like a scratching post

failing to show where it's at

i often think

of our bedroom apartment

overlooking the seine

playing grownups

yet painting it pink

what i would give

to be back there with you

feeling no pain

and being in sync

when he was little

girls' wet kisses

had him wipe lips and cheeks

in disgust

now he welcomes

a bit of spittle

as expedient ingredient of lust

the irish girl

or was she french

i never knew

she wouldn't talk

neat like a pearl

next on my bench

i tried to cue her

to please not walk

IV. SOME TIME AGO

we had posters of cars on our walls
and quite a few of models
as scantily clad as our moms allowed
somehow the two got muddled

she made him stutter
lose grip of the rudder
heart valves aflutter
brains turned to butter

entered my daydreams
affectionate stranger
never could figure out
who she was

he often spoke of different directions
all new ambitions went rapidly broke
afoul of long-enshrined predilections
his feigned resolve seemed like a joke

have i been walking this city's streets
with her on my mind but not my arm
this where wish with fantasy meets
i am so taken in by her charm

are there any good knights anymore
maybe they always were
figments of lore
or scoundrels with good pr

IV. SOME TIME AGO

you have no business
being this taught
and i have none anymore
being so caught

long time ago he had breaks in a row
thought he'd be favored forever
but over time we reap what we sow
karma returns and pulls the lever

summer rain shower in the backyard
dancing an hour under the spout
guiltily shrouded shyness was routed
they found what good life was about

spring was muted from my senses
could not stand as its brilliance grew
not let its fancy sweep past my fences
my love would have broken through
unrestrained and with nothing to do
then arrived you the girl who dances
with lust and passion that enhances
all the beauty that had made me blue

october campground on the coast
we are the only ones out there
you sleep deeply as you do most
innocent and without a care
i hear steps shuffling outside the tent
jump with a knife prepared to defend
it's the attendant collecting the rent

IV. SOME TIME AGO

she wrote i have kind hands
though ours had never touched

while she was getting
protractedly dressed
her roommate was letting
herself be impressed
in spite of his staunch retreating

she held for him
a passing passion
more like a whim
a seasonal fashion
soaking up popularity

in our youth we were busy exploring
and playing out our fantasies
then came awareness
and pain made us boring
indifference is a quiet disease

they had his beater
and her bed to share
turning in both with equal care

there was an endless pebbled beach
you were collecting crystal rocks
carefully assessing each
transporting them in your socks

IV. SOME TIME AGO

you see it was by smaller gestures
she demonstrated conditional trust
one day she cast off all her vestures
certain she had perforated my crust

your dress clung tightly
after the rain
still you skipped lightly
showing no pain
steam rising blithely
from you me and the seine

i first met love in higher education
a multi semester collision course

played and put away for now
but i know you will come back
music we made let us glean the tao
some day we'll get back on track

first single i bought
as boy of few years
instead of candy
still sweet to my ears

and all wisdom of the ages
was overturned with a flip of her hair
none left to seek between the pages
all he can think of is bite her ripe pear

IV. SOME TIME AGO

if we could insert us in younger selves
be that certain that new love dwells
after anguish around the next corner
unaware of the clench of the former
maybe this time it can meet us there

she loved to give me novelty kisses
one was like a strong-minded slug

sometimes i think
it would have been charming
trading in ink
for prehistoric farming
then i picture required arming

eating cherries
red vampire teeth
you arrange fairies
into a wreath
heaven in paris
we underneath

i left my time to hold her just once
now her eternity has me ensconced

faint memories of love recounted
trophies of beautiful ladies mounted
with fantasies that would've haunted
had they not been overtly flaunted

IV. SOME TIME AGO

the very moment i viewed music
as more than a technical challenge
it came to me and stayed
lesson learned for life and love

sitting alone far off the party
she doubted i knew her
from former leading roles

the song that i published
about your name
leaves me deprived
though it nurtures my fame
using it this way fills me with shame

she was a lost lyric
he could not recall
like dreams of flying
and then endless fall

he sometimes felt
like a tennis ball
and girls were
searing hot velcro

that fresh day in may
right after a rain
when young leaves and blossoms
had no fear of falling

IV. SOME TIME AGO

did he say gold or cold
it really doesn't matter

a bed so small
we had to spoon together
a love so big we did it anyway

guess she lost touch
or never had it
loved him too much
piercing soul and heart
he moved away
saying he regretted
not being ready to play his part

remember back when
we were singing and basking
children unhemmed
exploring and asking
joy without end
till we bought into masking

not having been there for you
some recollections never heal

we are the echoes of ancestors' pain
ungrateful they make us sound
ignorant egos lone cut off and vain
needles in haystacks unfound

IV. SOME TIME AGO

something remains
of who lived here before
undefined stains
on walls ceiling and floor
filth is the last notion parting

she was a decrepit miller's daughter
who helped and grew strong
pulling millstones' ore
worship the sun by a pond he saw her
and met his calling to ever adore

like an oyster revealing her pearl
she opened up to him no more a girl

in the days of simple pleasures
we sought buckeye treasures
felt their glistening veneer
leaped into heaves of leaves
breathed in fermented fall air
now such proximity is rare

he was predicting
he'd die in august
getting ready every year

why he complained
must i dream of her
i don't know even who she is

V. FRAME OF MIND

V. FRAME OF MIND

she wants to give the world
all she has got
unless demands are hurled
then she will not

I never understood why women's
number one wish in a man is smarts,
but when they want to signal a guy
they really like him they call him silly.

Happiness is a mechanism driving us
to improve ourselves and the world
around us, not just a matter of
attitude or accommodating practices.

Artists create nothing. They cannot help what is already there forcing them to give it expression at the risk of consuming them either way.

for good or bad we are not drawing
unchanging points or lines anymore

looking up to hot air balloons
all my idols have long flown

how can humanity escape itself

V. FRAME OF MIND

soldiers on all sides
are commonly good guys
unaware being played for their fears
told they are fighting ignoble ideas
reinforced as each one of them dies
meet reservations with blind deriding

crushes his dreams
so others won't do it
fearful he would not fit in

media is helping its insecure wards
fiercely brag of professional sports
signaling they too are virile players

challenged him
hit me
as if to prove
he was no different
from other men she knew

tribes are considerably more prone
to go crazy
than the average of their members

I dream of a world without fear of
harm, but then think those inclined
to inflict harm should have much
more such fear instilled in them.

how do i know
something with me is wrong
it's when i cannot find a song
or my darkness minds the bright
and i can't be told everything's alright

your love is shameless
i had been aimless
till you embarrassed
the hell out of me

you say you tie your hair in ratty tails
i only see wondrous beautiful braids
with strands of my sanity interwoven

will we keep fighting
forefathers' battles
drawing on who had them wronged
or finally refuse being led like cattle
realize
for what foremothers longed

each day she gave him
a chip of her heart
he played them all away

dating a model
took some courage
mainly on her part

V. FRAME OF MIND

you never take your love in context
the only thing that counts for you
he thought of you more as a conquest
to have a fling with and currently woo

what we need
versus what we want
what we reap
versus what we can't
what we keep
versus what we grant

when he too easily flies off the handle
she feels sorry offers wine and candle

i love the light
for giving me sight
so i can delight
in her turning me on
still night is my friend
who will be at hand
long after she's gone

sending bad feelings amplified back
hard as it is do not fall in this trap
reason and raise sights moving on

it's hard to unmask ridiculousness
without revealing humor

V. FRAME OF MIND

the best revenge

is to get off the bench

where injustice tries to demote you

minds resemble oceans

we only see tides waves and storms

stand reflecting at the fringes

many depths yet unexplored

often in dreams

you were calling my name

this has come true

but it's not the same

when you wake me to go to work

watching her walk
stuck the rhythm line
of every love song in his heart

she swears no matter
i'll be by your side
he cares she can better
tell wrong from right

you hurl your untamed mane
and it unfurls
curls cascading
in little whirls
girl you drive me insane

V. FRAME OF MIND

humanity's sanity is losing trust
soon doubt may reach us
and people we know
question them and us we must
even when expectations run low

demanding love's
like commanding the sun
you must go where it shines

your love's force
makes you let me be me
but i of course
want your fealty

KNOWING WON'T LET DARKNESS REIGN

love knows no shame

it is destined to aim

like tracks for a train

at fulfillment past bane

though the odds might be insane

some greatly suffer

treated well

thinking they don't deserve it

he calls her his rosette of cauliflower

she him her asparagus spear

feasting on meat is a concept too sour

thus vegan terms are used to endear

V. FRAME OF MIND

silence is only hurtful
if we expect sound

life's pretty low
with no high of love

is she just crazy
or madly in love

loving come what may
or throwing all away
nothing between to parlay

if gold were ubiquitous
we'd hold most precious
the soothing dullness of gray slate

tackling life as a transient form of art
seems tremendously daunting
and indecently flaunting
but with death haunting
and occupations we can't tell apart
we better get a start before we depart

you estrange by judging me
i can't won't revert who i used to be
all that should matter is now

V. FRAME OF MIND

I used to believe in the law of
averages until I tracked the frequency
by which I put on t-shirts in the dark
in reverse and inside out.

our minds are mere nets
catching floating ideas
some pull us along
between our ears

this is not going to work she opined
he responded that's ok
it was just play i had in mind
paired with one or another perk

flowers bloomed
and begged for rain
without it they cried we are doomed
heaven brimmed
you're complaining in vain
i'm not in charge of earthly pain

who are we apart from all that blings
from accounts purses wallets things
not counting our dominions
appendages and tools
are we come-to-life opinions
of self-centered shallow fools
proud of experience and schools
without knowing what passion brings
do we dare spread our spirit's wings

V. FRAME OF MIND

some women are like butterflies

others gnawing caterpillars

tease you to rise or chew you to size

bringers of life or determined killers

those who can't lose well

will not do well winning

a life described in first and last times

and repetition in between

one can be tired of various tenses

measures success
by how much she is loved
without returning the favor

i often thought i heard her name
by birds announced before she came
in joy and reverie not as a warning

this awkward bloke
is going for broke
out of his yoke to impress you
he's scary nice
so put on the ice
tell him no dice and not to harass you

V. FRAME OF MIND

leaved forest paths remind me
of fragile light movements
that are for me no more
snow-covered trail ruts grind me
recalling grooves that i adore

holding beliefs we need any leaders
short-circuit imprints on our minds

silence is not nothing
it's the courage to hear
even when there is no sound
it helps us develop our ear
for the event music can be found

still can't decide
between fact and fiction
guess it depends
on which disappoints

This guitar is so beautiful I hardly
care what she sounds like - which is a
mistake in picking guitars or women.

mettle exposed to air and rains
will eventually run down drains
or turn into brittle scattered dust
still i let oxygen moisten my veins
knowing well it will make me rust

Humanity's stance on itself and Earth
is so upside down, it might benefit
from turning the globe outside in.
Then we could always see it and each
other and maybe pay more attention.

pay attention to misread words
they are closed-captions of your soul

In limiting ourselves to rhymes, we
sentence expressions to striking but
finite formality dictated by accidents
of similar-sounding phrases. The
context of concepts matters more.

we live on islands
of different sizes
till one realizes
we all come from the sea

my love my life without you
would never be the same
still it would be about you
lived somehow but in vain

not quite sure
why she calls me now pumpkin
was nearly certain
i'm to her a gourd

V. FRAME OF MIND

his ideal of the opposite sex
changed as he progressed through life
still he left his dates perplexed
asking for everything in a wife

man's just a guest in women's homes
no matter how he shares or roams
or how important he thinks he is
no home qualities are his

when she's in his sight
he acts like a knight
but there's too much white
in his eyes of terror

close with her
it's almost too much
barred from her
nothing's enough
he'll only rest when he's gone

cherry blossom honeymoon
you could not focus on us
something about your mother

she hugged the lilac bush
just like a person
thank you for making
my mind smell so good

V. FRAME OF MIND

she shook him up
the self-confessed
self-contained
and self-assured

her body
mellowness
and spikes
did things to him
he had not felt the likes

reinforce children's
sense of beauty
and all else will fall into place

lying we claim to have this feeling
fully aware the feeling has us

time has the air of passing and dying
we never know we are safe

more ice on mars's north pole
than its counterpart on earth
change of climate and perspective

minds that can't see common ground
must join hands to build a bridge

V. FRAME OF MIND

i want the sun to singe me
another coat of skin
want rushing wind and water
to strip me of my sin
and start anew with you

he often wished
she would switch positions
ride motorbikes with him in the back

stammering words
unfit for emotions
or visions of us
playing in my mind

she has him going
for days at a time
until he's exhausted
and comes back to her

what a strangely brand-new day
everything seems to be fired clay
hot to the touch
and lifelessly hardened

letters i write are meant to cool
searing regret
absence burns in this fool
until we rekindle the fire

V. FRAME OF MIND

her derogations upon his body

deemed him depraved

desiring hers

when he shaped up

she continued them oddly

as an incentive but he felt worse

fractured glass hearts

give rise to rainbows

as the sun reflects on their scars

every time you think

you're someone

you are the opposite too

she keeps admitting
i needed that
unacquainted with the fact
she is the only one giving

watch for the things
people claim to be awful
when really they are
miraculous nature

A rising number of people prefer not
to be confronted with themselves,
thus refusing ownership, opportunity,
growth, awareness, and fulfillment.

V. FRAME OF MIND

boundaries are made to keep
evil fear or carelessness at bay
or to enable them

he's hardest on the ones he loves
to dissuade them
from taking advantage
of what he perceives
an embarrassing weakness for them

i do not feel like i am myself quite
more a transparent abandoned ghost
who long ago died
but still is holds the post

smiling i'm writing
she asks what is this
memorializing
fleeting bliss

where will his love go
when she's not around
will he claim he's taken
though opportunities abound

i often wonder
if i lay with you
would i still care
to know what's false or true

VI.
CRITIQUE

VI. CRITIQUE

do not peak

if for you it's not meant

do not speak

when you don't understand

do not seek

what's inevident

fall in line with government

speckled reality

waive flags and sigh

let your lead criminal

murder and lie

print in annals

he was a good guy

only used cruelty

saving your pie

for once stop rambling
about how you feel
listen acknowledge respond

why we wear hard clothes and shoes
why we are settling in with the blues
why we suffer unpursued passions
why we are recruited like hessians
advertising and selling out

watch people pushing indication
they are this or that
directly or through act
often more posture than inclination

VI. CRITIQUE

carped about nobody hearing him
when he was not listening to himself

defending a thesis
to be in the fold
academic omen

don't brag about love just show it

We show persistent uncertainty in
our right to self-govern although its
transfer to others courts disaster.

stringent rules
for boys she had kept
went overboard
as soon as we met

your skin
as smooth as sanded marble
you heart
as cold and hard as well

badmouthing happiness
unwise unreal
just goes to show
how left out they feel

VI. CRITIQUE

buying evinces unhappiness
with a current position
and expecting better success
through an acquisition

the right to self-determination
deeply revered by civilization
until it irks rulers of a nation
then it is scrapped without hesitation

what can one say
about rubber stamp people
except that one wishes
they'd run out of ink

it's not that we don't care enough
but what we care about is partly nuts

Threats to a society benefit those
relied on to address them because
they derive increased legitimacy and
powers from this position. Conflicting
incentives and reduced control ensue.

machine intelligence in the air
why can't computers self-repair
or often don't know ills that ail them
frenzied owners pull out their hair
forced to hang on in spite of mayhem

VI. CRITIQUE

don't wear my shirts
as impromptu nightgowns
i scare too easily
waking next to me

millions of children are dying
while we debate who was lying
as if it were the most pressing fact
it's no excuse for our failure to act

rebuff by women makes him irate
tender won't make his anger abate
they should not be so easy to bait
in his mind he won't ever be enough

judging others

we always judge ourselves

love you

have got me

to the brink

of daring to tell you

what i think

of your directing

my food and drink

midriff shirts or skirts too short

for flying public places or work

due to observers' mental dirt

VI. CRITIQUE

be wary of opinions
not interested in yours

thieves challenge us
to make our bets
on stepping stones
past whipped up angry waters
we notice they are hydra's heads
still nobody questions or bothers

she calls her parts
by silly little names
he asks to kindly
not ridicule his

Why do we think people arguing out loud with themselves are irrational? Maybe the rest of us fear this critical dialogue that might be necessary or helpful to straighten out our minds.

culture of people
is quickly assessed
by what there is for breakfast

The greatest human failing is wanting to be right. While useful and thus excusable, it can easily cause us to be wrong without the recourse of doubt.

VI. CRITIQUE

people once used to
dress for their roles
downturns of manners
have taken their tolls

gullible sheep
wolves ready to pounce
here goes humanity
down further rounds

I admit to judging people. I judge them by how differently they act depending on whether they want something or are on notice to give.

Tribalism, its promoters, organizers,
beneficiaries, cheerleaders, and
spectators damage a society, allowing
lowest instincts and infamies to rule.

she does not like him
for having had a life
till she broke into view
not enough she's now his wife
she sets him up to search anew

a lot less bad would happen
if people would not allow
being directed by others

VI. CRITIQUE

say thank you each day
on many occasions
directed to and from you
this either points to
facts you should cherish
or irony you ought to mend

commodity people
ready for scanners

fearing a void
to simply be
stuffing our life with activity
wailing we don't have time

common sense's death

is not surprising

since most of our others

are atrophied from catering

hobbyist sport statisticians

spending life-long childhoods

to shadow teams and players

splitting them up in likes and dislikes

Children's opinions are habitually

ridiculed and marginalized because

their brains are not yet developed to

cease asking probing questions.

VI. CRITIQUE

By claiming that the truth of matters
cannot be obtained, we may give in to
false interpretations - and even more
so by claiming truth can be obtained.

much of what she says is wrong
but he finds it endearing
she's got him bleeding on her prong
apologetic for smearing
another fool in love

the sole searching way
she knew how to gauge love
was by cruelty she or he would suffer

she likes to hook
her legs into mine
as if to make sure
i won't run away

her favorite poems
are of people broken
since most she knows
are a gooey mess

the new in you
will tide him over
until the next lover
appears in his view

VI. CRITIQUE

she says love is a numbers game
with most of us settling on too few

politics and sports
are often the same
people choose teams
tribal idiocy in reams
others profit from the game

fluid existence clotting
old men favor plotting
adversity and war
jealous of young life
they burn its vigor in strife

most of their worries

and passed-on stories

projections on others

that give them covers

for justifying themselves

principles are broken

innocence upturned

humanity a token

till victory is earned

lasting desire is unfulfilled

since we soon tire

when tension is killed

VII.
DESPAIR

VII. DESPAIR

lonely in essence

despite effervescence

people watching her like a show

and she puts it on from head to toe

you robbed me

of all resolve to be strong

first when i met you

and now that you're gone

all books and letters

are not enough

to soak up

all the world's tears

november leaves
avoid in me
the need to fall myself

after he said it
she sensed implosions
of all the stars they had
gazed together
hurling swirling into a black hole

those without love
deem it often stupid
cursing not having it
with all their smarts

VII. DESPAIR

flights to roam

when night inks houses

drowns out the loud

no soul is about

only strays and i

cannot go home

no matter how we try

you gave a concert

no one came

getting your feelings hurt

part of the game

but having arrived

it's just the same

nobody says a word

silenced by fame

the forest is still

its silence seems shrill

knowing you are somewhere in it

searched many hours

now my mind devours

alternate hope and hopelessness

seeing a mitt and shreds of your dress

not to return

can be a blessing

letting long gone

gaunt spirits sleep

once we do

no window dressing

spares us the burn

of wounds running deep

VII. DESPAIR

expanding voiding loneliness

within as without

silence equals shout

you clamor you're under

untold pressure

but that's how most gems are made

they don't talk a lot

though each still got

a mute conversation

within with the other

locked resignation

that still does bother

peak moment in his disbelief
she sneaked out on him
just like a thief

she sings no more
he doesn't play
not much before
they've got nothing to say
even for sadness pretense or pay

listen she warned the child
you cannot sing
confidence harmed
a continual sting

VII. DESPAIR

why did people settle here
in this forsaken land
where must they have hailed from
what could they not bear
fleeing instead of taking a stand

nothing could tell me
you were not mine
until i saw you stand in a line
of girls with backstage passes

losing you makes me
seriously question
will i ever be found

life never caught up
with advertisements

don't ask
what in you she loves
she might realize
not having a clue
don't tell
what you see in her
she might despair
living up to it

i do not recognize the world
without you in it anymore

VII. DESPAIR

shaving your head
for the operation
you joke
why don't they just
go through the ears

glorious sunset
to end all days
will we still fear the dark

hell is not a place
it's when our minds
have nowhere to go
to escape their demons

the macaroni heart

she once gave him

is dissolving

in boiling tears

smoking drink and excess

slightly preferred to being dead

after his children left home and wed

and so did all beloved exes

life sometimes feels

like a backlogged jackhammer

hitting each time

smooth concrete has cured

VII. DESPAIR

shakes you awake
and sobs i'm leaving
that's not the take
you got from last evening
when she said she was
not mad anymore

a silent touch
is still too much
after what he said

gaunt scruffy man
in a suit from the eighties
waving a mirror to catch his ghosts

if we refuse to follow our dreams
we must fight them haunting us back
they seep into each unchecked crack
bursting us at the seams

no need to say
you don't love me no more
i felt your stare
when my card bounced at the store

my love once had me freely breathing
then knocked all air out of me leaving
quipped at the door got to get away
maybe we talk some other day

VII. DESPAIR

spring or summer was not her season
panicking without apparent reason
when all except for her flourished

binge watching
can bridge a lot of bore
yet series end
giving way to void more

she handles herself
with full consciousness
of her beguiling intoxication
uses it with intent to bless
still leaving utter deprivation

lays herself open into his hands
though she wantonly hurts him
can't be vindictive
or take a hard stance
she is the quench
for which he is thirsting

why must he think
of a girl named colton
never knew anyone
with that name

dehumanizing tides are rising
drowning us in them is unsurprising

VII. DESPAIR

i cannot help it that i love you
i tried to fib but it is too true
my heart insists to tell i think of you
even if it starts a hell i will rue

her name or meme
are nowhere to be found
i guess one day we all disappear

claims not to mind
if he sees other women
trying to save what little she can
but she will not give all of her to him
he never was nor will be her man

without pauses
even the most beautiful conditions
become insufferable

passing not passing
the terrors of time
haunt our sanity
so to be fine
we cling to vanity
as a life line

mostly they fight
to dispel the fright
of nothing to say anymore

VII. DESPAIR

times i got no words in me
and the rest wants to fight or flee
no song or smile not even for you
no empathy is getting through
that's when your love matters most

we're living in a film negative
with insufficient exposure
that's why there's never closure

the years without tears
had left her brittle
with no seed to moisten
for a new life

she is familiar with her sadness
waiting for fall to agree with her
his silly demeanor makes her laugh
how dare he spring in and interfere

my love's not conditioned
on whether you love me
and yet its fate is
determined by you

a girl i am not acquainted with
and likely will never meet
can't possibly ever know from this riff
my words were laid at her feet

VII. DESPAIR

publishing diaries

of souls within

wasting in prison

their only way out

A whole generation of writers in the
romantic era struggled and could not
change the ugly heart of creeping
modernity - and perished of it.

don't keep asking

why i am still here

there is no good reason

except spit(t)ing fear

KNOWING WON'T LET DARKNESS REIGN

in the darkest hour
where late and early gather
her mind and heart devour
all else for not having a father

i heard the man upstairs had passed
after a garbage container was cast
his relatives want none of his stuff
ending buried or burned seems rough

all the things i should not say
and parts of me i should not show
you'd love my fictional version to stay
the one i invented to make it a go

VII. DESPAIR

dutiful essence of an archangel
aiming to fuse sacrifice to her heart
begs for no mercy as lashes knell
passion's hell extinguished that part

It used to be people died because
they grew tired from the challenges of
living. Nowadays it appears more
they die from tiring of not living.

she was never more alone
than with those
who should make her at home
or with whom she was trying

my love has left me
a rose on the bed
i should be happy
instead just feel dread

stars warm and bright
forever lonesome
spreading light
until they burn out

working buying
still there we are
stuck with the self-respect
we have earned

VII. DESPAIR

she kept the shirt which he last wore
carrying the scent
before her heart tore

she was a nonperson
barely present
pain in her semblance
straining to be birthed

sense of duty on a shelf
keeping diaries from falling
she begins to hate herself
there's nothing in them
she could be trawling

she's in my dreams
even when i'm with you
just a guitar now babe
please don't be blue
every man needs a side passion

she was turning his life into hers
adjunct existence robotic burbs
sometimes he wished all was burning

he's mostly trying to forget
what life has in store
by keeping a pet
which has not given up on him yet

VIII.
REGRET

VIII. REGRET

i don't see the moon anymore
your glow eclipsed it forever
even if we parted
i could not regard it
with all my heart

every moment leaves me
you were just one of them
mutual stare
embarrassing rare
missing a chance again

the least we can do
is nothing irreversible

she asks pointedly
whether i miss her
or am merely lonely

feats tend to turn us
prize winning asses
until a lack of luck
makes us step down some classes

i should not be ungrateful
to agonize and ask what if
i could have shared
the moment was fateful
made a connection not fallen adrift

VIII. REGRET

parting she said
that she thought i was smart
as if this had made less a fool of me

back on tours my heart wakes up
to disappointment that i cut
circulation with yours
the bleeding won't stop
no matter the dressing
well-deserved but still depressing
lost love is an ill with no cures

some ridicule those sentimental
but few die with a smirk on their face

it's not so much now
that i want to be with you
but if you left too
my heart might break
can't disavow
it's only loneliness at stake

love you call i should come to bed
but a pall of doubt plagues my head
is there enough to be happy

times i don't dare touching you
for fear of disturbing
the beauty you are

VIII. REGRET

winks of your eyes
flutter brightly on
voice fragments echo
though you're long gone
what i would give for a day

the radio plays
this song we both love
hurt flees our bodies
soft conquers rough
why couldn't this last forever

waking up lately disoriented
your compassion has left my side

i'm just a fool whose judgment is poor
still you want me to forgive you for
not being what i had hoped you were

he loves country life she fashion
he writes the checks she's cashing
a difference in passion

playing guitar is calming my fears
now that you're far night only hears
our impassioned lonesome duet
your song still echoes soft in my ears
stars project our wave-bound tears
i carry you in my memories to bed

VIII. REGRET

aspects of us become wondrous
when we don't have them anymore
jokers tend to get ponderous
wondering what they are joking for

stretched between pins
rare animal skins
hollowed out bodies of nature
since this was never among our sins
shame is not worth a wager

losing each other and ourselves
we put dreams upon separate shelves
from where they keep staring at us

i'm sad when people sneer at my sight
but then feel guilty of silly pride
say guess that's the cost of being right

leaving
twirled curls
bestuck with flowers
turning now
won't wait
till i'm out of sight

some day soon
after many suffered
she won't allow one single more

VIII. REGRET

she sends me a rose
and a face throwing kisses
though my rhymes are prose
their words mostly misses

the things we lose
in us in others
dig in our souls
expanding holes

when she first fell for him
he loved her as if trying
to split her in half
he over time succeeded

174 KNOWING WON'T LET DARKNESS REIGN

she naturally lights me
and makes me see my spots
sometimes furor bites me
because there are lots

give and take
one thousand months
or shorter
that's what we've got to work with

giving up chances
unless you are certain
still can be foolish
unless you are right

VIII. REGRET

everything stuck in perennial winter
i can't tell what that's all about
want to spring back
when things were simpler
we were then just starting out

talking to homeless folks
made his friends queasy
like they could catch
their affliction through him

he could not say
she's the love of his life
until all had about faded away

lost faith in ourselves
or never had it
invented gods
who don't much trust us either

when i picture you my love
you're absent-minded
watching the sea
is it me you are thinking of
or is your heart blinded
by my last spree

every time we give power away
ends in heartbreak and dismay

VIII. REGRET

some morning suns
chase shadows off
some burn fantasies
not seized enough
both lingering from you
being absent with me

if we knew how
we hurt one another
would we sufficiently care

best friend
heart worm
that ate from inside

some people continue
right after they're hit
others see fit
to from then on drone
how they've been wronged
and pick on dead bone

his regret
is a summer's dream
he could not in fall forget

you will remember this shameful part
strangles my heart
when angry words are hurting her

VIII. REGRET

you never claimed to not burn me
and i was fervently hoping for that
then you decided to turn me
till i was done and rendered all fat

you say i don't know you
and maybe i don't
but you've played it safe
making sure i won't

your blood was free
so they took it
you died for the glee
of the crooked

she looks at him melancholically
like death on an early soul
he could be hers eventually
pouncing now will exact a toll

every time i'm leaving
sensing a bit what death must be like
there is no way retrieving
the loss still i go and take a hike

so many gestures half-hearted
our faint troubles not worthy at all
better still not to have bothered
now we contribute to someone's fall

VIII. REGRET

i mourn each working day we lost
time we don't share but rather give
each one comes at increasing cost
but you say we have to live

after all vicious you put her through
she would still take your hand
not in forgiveness but merely to end

many loves test us in finding our way
full of hurdles and unseen traps
others appear much more rewarding
walk us gently into their gardening
where we get planted as married saps

you're really nice
but cannot have me
a doubtful prize even to myself

you know the letters
you never sent
or the feelings
that were not meant
all this still existed
because i missed it

her bold demeanor's enamored rage
challenged him to turn a page
instead he closed the book

VIII. REGRET

i'm sad she said
setting satin sills
with votive candles
then took some pills
in hopes of lighting
his way back to her

all those years we meet after work
i am not sure what she does by day

four-letter words
we should not say
are nothing compared
to the one we won't

meant to betray her
though dove-tailing peg
she still fancies him
will even beg
to answer her prayer
be her soothsayer
be her mistake
make her future dim

i wrote you a song
that went all wrong
it came out wry
instead of praising
to boot a bullseye
instead of grazing
about your wearing a thong

IX.
ANTICIPATION

IX. ANTICIPATION

what can he stress
she won't already know
paying attention to his intentions
will she insist he bare his soul
is this a dare he'll pay any toll

come you blessing angel i can see
lift me hold me tumble with me
heaven won't mind you have fallen

the more she holds dear
the more grows her fear
that she might lose
without ability to bear

confident attitude
part of a game
where you act rude
when i ask your name
testing my courage
and threshold of pain
in really getting to know you

she moans take me
he doesn't know where

when's the time that you let go
i've been waiting but i don't know
you're still afraid you will be judged

IX. ANTICIPATION

give it a whirl baby
don't wait and see
the dress the hat
your life
and me

never sure she'll be staying
he challenges her to leave
to make her commit or cut his grief
what does it take for him to believe
there is no cure for what he's saying

mocking him has a ceding price
she gladly pays after teasing his eyes

KNOWING WON'T LET DARKNESS REIGN

seeing how guys leer at you

tells me that my dreams came true

or that nightmares are just beginning

time flies

collect the highs

obliterate the pain

soon it's all the same

but we're not just there yet

i know we are not meant to last

an episode a blink a blast

let's try to sparkle while we're cast

and see how far we get streaming

IX. ANTICIPATION

i know we are not meant to win
still let's be true and not give in
decry the vain and name the lies
so we stand sight of mirrored eyes

an in your face world
but your beautiful secrets
keep me believing
i have not yet seen all
especially if you won't call

pleasure of modern life
snuggled in bed
writing to friends we never met

every day in evening hue
come what may i go to the strand
hold out my hand and call to the sea
that i am still much bluer than she

i cannot wait to cannot wait

wears a skirt like a daffodil
and a white blouse
as we climb the hill
spring in my step
yet hope petals will fall
she planned ahead of course
knowing it all

IX. ANTICIPATION

what if the bright star
i revere from afar
is just a hole
in a cardboard box
that may be right
but its intrepid light
must then arise
from farther beyond

earphoned late walks
on summer evenings
grass heavy roses
sprinklers' hiss
warmly lit windows
banter of families
one day it will be like this

Humanity rationalizes its existence
through machines until they
rationalize humanity for theirs.

daydreams beset
by your scent looks and ways
though since we met
it has only been days
i think i can't live without you

crispness of fall
has a prompting air
quiet times call
how did you prepare

IX. ANTICIPATION

all our lives
getting ready for what
finding already
we missed our putt

and as we lay down
the day's tribulations
will we continue
to hold hands in dreams

most of the time
he would not get started
for fear of what would be
after the end

Physics gradually prove time, space,
matter as superficial phenomena on
the path to their underlying truth,
which we may not be able to grasp.

keep going she whips
as i come around
we think the same way
but with different directions

the way she manhandled
cut flowers to vases
signaled to him
quick coverage of bases

IX. ANTICIPATION

high pitch and low growl

of crackling tension

should someone around

just mention her sight

or that she might be here tonight

their hopes of sunbathing

head to toes

were doused by scathing mosquitoes

problems arose

when her love was spineless

this time she'll keep at least

some of her thorns

she has me thinking
our kite will be sinking
unless a harsh wind constantly blows

mom drummed her ears
not to be easy
undeterred years
he has held out hope kept
but now begs her to finally please see
that it is time to settle the debt

molten she lays
tonight's fire will pass
morning will find her obsidian glass

IX. ANTICIPATION

turns off the lights

then on a candle

turning to me

wondering what i can handle

stupid she claims

but her eyes sign approval

a summer fair's dream

thunderstorm steam rises

carneys shout out prizes rides careen

children beam pairs prance to be seen

show of mild vices no one looks mean

bliss seems too big a couple of sizes

anyone saying that morning breaks

should get up early

watch sun's dewy haze

lovingly gently envelop the earth

out of her way

yet keeps walking by

her tease is subtle

but smile too wry

telling of thoughts i should notice

her poise of pronouncing

my name every time

as if she cares how it feels

IX. ANTICIPATION

and when our day
approaches its end
we won't have much to say
walk the short distance
hand in hand
knowing we went all the way

sunday morning sun rays
on dirty window panes
my mind's on perfection
just one day without stains

first notes define
the whole symphony

she taped two pillows
behind the headboard

she doesn't like help
that's not necessary
pushing away
his chivalrous gestures
under suspicions
they may not last

i've turned to distant sentiments
from boredom of which you speak
attempting hard to mend the fence
that once generated mystique

IX. ANTICIPATION

she dresses to signal
don't come too close
fearing her sting's like a bee's

unsteady eyes like an untamed doe's
driven to shelter by winter snows
the trust she grants is tense
no false move or she leaps the fence
keeping you on your toes

all she wears
is these flimsy wrap dresses
daring her beau
to pull the bow

fascinating and baffling at once
the girl who is nothing like him
will they fuse by love heat ensconced
or be eternally fighting

the purple mood you bring to me
bears thousand-fold yet undiscovered
i want nothing else just want to be
the one who has you forever bothered

shhhhhhh she says
and points a finger up
has magic ways to make talk stop
and enter deeper communications

IX. ANTICIPATION

showing her body a sacrilege
born from fair fear
of too much worship
and the powers she could wield

tip of an iceberg
she faces love to melt her
keeps nine tenths reserved
to not thaw too fast

he is considering working out
for landing a hard-body chick
even if that were a total rout
she would have played a neat trick

shrouded within
her rose petal skin
gossamer blossom
reveries of soaring

asked me you have somewhere to be
yes right here
she nodded i see

parts of you soften
when you let me touch
still you think often
that i don't care much
hurting them or your feelings

IX. ANTICIPATION

my heart's bulkhead
is loaded with springs
so is my bed
among other things

retinas seared
from seeing her naked
blind love is leading him
into her fire

if grasshoppers knew
where they will land
would pleasures be few
and life taste bland

though a stranger to her own body
and its offensive desires
scared by temporariness
she submits to its fire

so this is what you do my love
when nobody watches you play
i find it to be a treasure trove
for things we can do to relay

love she asks
would you like more tea
i basked in her attention to me
likely she's just a great waitress

IX. ANTICIPATION

ever since when he was a mere boy
valued old clay roofs on houses high
after hearing the tiles one could buy
were each formed on a woman's thigh

pending between and waiting for bliss
wishing our pains were over
we fail to grasp the gist of this
waste in trials not to be sober

i consider that time you bit me
when i was trying to plant a kiss
or incidents when you would hit me
volatile clouds in longed for bliss

to test his pestering right to a stop
and prove he was unappealing
she did request he kiss her shoes
just bending without kneeling
any attempt appeared certain to lose
yet when he pulled her leg up
she thought it best to give it a rest
and confess to her long-held feeling

you are attempting to save us both
by claiming you will betray me

he lived his life first in anticipation
and then again in desperation

X.
HEALING

X. HEALING

indian holocaust two continents
but those are former colonial crimes
now we are in different times
no earned pardon or true repentance
still reveling in their blood and fines

No medals are due for abandoning
the abduction, captivity, spiritual and
physical murder, rape, torture, and
brainwashing of tribes and nations,
women, men, children and legally
freeing their survivors when the
resulting concentration camps we call
reservations, plantations, ghettos,
slums, favelas, projects, public
housing, inner cities still trap them.

That one can be happy by so deciding
is similarly absurd as becoming rich
by pronouncement. Resolve merely
activates an often-difficult process.

Happiness is a fickle condition that
results from the correlation between
the entireties of our self and our
setting as well as among their details.

lessons to stick with
what one likes to do
made me conclude
that for me this is you

X. HEALING

is it time to criticize each other
or is our love's coverage so abundant
that it can safely envelop all we are
including our weaknesses and failings
and let us occur in our wish to please

we can only truly be free
if we let each other be
and build upon consensus

suddenly broke into my heart
trying to make it her home
i was not stoked right from the start
but love now won't leave me alone

years kindly let me slowly forget
the flash of heat right when we met
and the long blizzard that followed
pain has mellowed brittled hollowed
still unforgiving but no more upset

we like to rest on good we've done
compile a sum as if we could outrun
the evil we've done with accounting

love unlocks hearts
that's how growth starts
helping minds grasp
different perspectives

X. HEALING

You can't force people into your life.
Live it with those who voluntarily
contribute to your happiness and
remain open to others joining.

sensing you
makes me make drugs in my head
so i forget reservations i had

hearts are not built
to be whole after breaking
just to scar over
the mark of their staking
once it has been removed

not being too good
to befriend anybody

enduring love
a reinforcing echo of itself

being human means negotiating
helplessness and unwillingness

times when cloaked pain
makes him throw all away
she blocks the path to the bin

X. HEALING

The world would heal if every
community with an existential
surplus helped another of similar size
whose existence is threatened.

your kiss my flame
thaws much of the ice
the world instills with endless lies
to cover carelessness

i stopped my prayers
relying on others
all the more joy
when love comes around

here we are so many years later
leapt over scars to love even greater
we veered far must think a spectator
yet just sparred to join even straighter

only take heed what others think
if they have care for you in mind
don't ration passion and soulful kin
will find love support and join you

must not keep our human side
from following its bliss
steadily polish its lumen bright
happiness builds like this

www.ingramcontent.com/pod-product-compliance
Lightning Source LLC
Chambersburg PA
CBHW032109090426
42743CB00007B/289